NEWCASTLE/BLOODAXE POETRY SERIES: 12

SEAN O'BRIEN:
JOURNEYS TO THE INTERIOR

NEWCASTLE/BLOODAXE POETRY SERIES

1: Linda Anderson & Jo Shapcott (eds.)
Elizabeth Bishop: Poet of the Periphery

2: David Constantine: *A Living Language*
NEWCASTLE / BLOODAXE POETRY LECTURES

3: Julia Darling & Cynthia Fuller (eds.)
The Poetry Cure

4: Jo Shapcott: *The Transformers*
NEWCASTLE / BLOODAXE POETRY LECTURES
[Delayed title: now due 2013]

5: Carol Rumens: *Self into Song*
NEWCASTLE / BLOODAXE POETRY LECTURES

6: Desmond Graham: *Making Poems and Their Meanings*
NEWCASTLE / BLOODAXE POETRY LECTURES

7: Jane Hirshfield: *Hiddenness, Uncertainty, Surprise*
NEWCASTLE / BLOODAXE POETRY LECTURES

8: Ruth Padel: *Silent Letters of the Alphabet*
NEWCASTLE / BLOODAXE POETRY LECTURES

9: George Szirtes: *Fortinbras at the Fishhouses*
NEWCASTLE / BLOODAXE POETRY LECTURES

10: Fiona Sampson: *Music Lessons*
NEWCASTLE / BLOODAXE POETRY LECTURES

11: Jackie Kay, James Procter & Gemma Robinson (eds.)
Out of Bounds: British Black & Asian Poets

12: Sean O'Brien: *Journeys to the Interior*
NEWCASTLE / BLOODAXE POETRY LECTURES

NEWCASTLE/BLOODAXE POETRY LECTURES

In this innovative series of public lectures at Newcastle University, leading contemporary poets speak about the craft and practice of poetry to audiences drawn from both the city and the university. The lectures are then published in book form by Bloodaxe, giving readers everywhere the opportunity to learn what the poets themselves think about their own subject.

NEWCASTLE/BLOODAXE POETRY SERIES: 12

SEAN O'BRIEN

Journeys to the Interior

Ideas of England in Contemporary Poetry

NEWCASTLE / BLOODAXE POETRY LECTURES

BLOODAXE BOOKS

ISBN: 978 1 85224 932 8

First published 2012 by
Department of English Literary & Linguistic Studies,
Newcastle University,
Newcastle upon Tyne NE1 7RU,
in association with
Bloodaxe Books Ltd,
Highgreen,
Tarset,
Northumberland NE48 1RP.

www.bloodaxebooks.com
For further information about Bloodaxe titles
please visit our website or write to
the above address for a catalogue.

Supported by
**ARTS COUNCIL
ENGLAND**

Cover design: Neil Astley & Pamela Robertson-Pearce.

Printed in Great Britain by
Bell & Bain Limited, Glasgow, Scotland.

Contents

As Deep as England

Ladies and Gentlemen, I hope you will forgive me if in this brief series of lectures I range quite widely, raising more questions than I seek to be able to answer, moving backwards and forwards in time, perhaps making connections without being able to pursue their implications properly. I've had to leave almost everything out. The subject, 'Ideas of England in Contemporary Poetry' is a large one, and it is also an area in which my own work as poet is engaged. So I'm partly on the inside of it myself. I am trying to find out what I think about it. If I knew the answer precisely, I might not be writing these lectures.

What does England mean? Well, as they say, if you have to ask... Yet it seems we do, perhaps especially in this period of rapid economic and social change, when the remains of the postwar settlement are impatiently dismantled and even to declare / accept / embrace a state of past-imperial modesty seems to be staking too large a claim on the world's attention and that of the markets who now govern us in all but name.

It could be objected that 'England' and 'Englishness' are not in themselves helpful ideas, that they resist clarification and contain too many internal contradictions, that the best way to understand a maze is perhaps not to go into it in the first place. But as I say, I am already inside the maze, imaginatively speaking, and have been at least since first I began to read and write poetry over forty years ago. My concern is with the workings of the imagination, which is not quite the same thing as the facts. The contradictions and paths into the mire and the grimpen, the dead ends and false trails, are part of the imagined England in which we live.

The poets with whom I began to read and study and write

poetry – Ted Hughes and T.S. Eliot – are both heavily invested in ideas of England which, though in some ways very different from each other, also have common ground in an enchanted or metaphysical notion of the place itself. So too does the poet who followed close on their heels in my reading, W.H. Auden, again ostensibly very different from the other two but drawn to the same ground, the common ground, perhaps, of their being. Many years later when I was writing a play about English Fascism in the 1920s and 30s, *Keepers of the Flame*, the hero found the image of what he wished to speak for at the heart of a wood in his native Northumberland: the resulting song was to bring him both fame and torment.

All interpretations, he may have felt, are misinterpretations. It may be too that in the individual and the collective imagination some places seem more England than others. It might be reasonable to suspect that dwellers south of a line running from, say, Stratford to London, feel themselves to be authentically English in a way that their neighbours to northwards seem to them not to be. And it's hardly necessary to remind an audience in Newcastle of the widespread instinctive sense in the North that *here* is clearly different from *down there* – yet at the same time it is England, perhaps for a northerner the *essential* presiding England, history notwithstanding. At one time not so long ago, some people liked to identify themselves as Northumbrians, but that making of an exception was also a claim to original authenticity, to having been in some sense here before the Normans, who are definitely 'not from round here'. The facts may argue differently, but England is a subject where the power of facts is quite limited. We are in the realm of belief and identity. The North, of course, still disproportionately supplies the armed forces with recruits – partly for economic reasons but partly too from identification with something almost beyond articulation that finds its most powerful emotional expression on occasions of national mourning and remembrance.

This lecture was written in part on Remembrance Sunday. There has been a good deal of public discussion this year about the wearing of poppies – by the England football team, by BBC presenters, by everyone else. There have been a lot of oughts about, a lot of they-should-be-made-to's. I have just read a news item from which I learn that some people are wearing larger poppies, or diamond encrusted poppies – presumably to indicate that they care more about the fallen than those who put their coppers in a street-seller's tin.

Where I live, spare diamonds are in relatively short supply, but on the way to the local churchyard for the ceremony of Remembrance I passed a teenage girl wearing a poppy pinned to her hat like a fashion accessory, and another with a poppy in her hair. I wasn't wearing a poppy myself, but my upbringing was traditional enough for me to have wondered momentarily if someone should suggest that they should put the poppy on the lapel, where it belongs. What someone? Where what belongs? Belongs to whom? In any case, what does the poppy now symbolise? Is it different from the blue cornflower worn by the French? I realised that, as so often happens by indirect routes, I was thinking about Englishness.

My attention was then distracted by further matters of protocol, manners, or as the current cant term has it, 'appropriateness', by the sight of the elegant fortyish companion of a uniformed army colonel, making her way through the drizzle, furiously chewing gum. Good job she wasn't playing the bugle.

The event itself went off quite smoothly, though numbers were down because of the rain. The recent riots were also said to have failed to ignite in the North East because it was raining. As people walked home afterwards, they passed houses with flags of St George displayed in the upper windows. Ten years ago hardly anyone would have known a flag of St George from a hole in the pavement, but ardent flag-wielders from the English Defence League were recently arrested in large numbers for trying to attack the anti-capitalist demonstrators encamped at St Paul's Cathedral. If it was necessary for the EDL to have a purpose other than a public ruck, it was presumably to defend England, but from what and in whose name? From the bankers? On the bankers' behalf?

England is in crisis, it seems. Who speaks for England? The famous phrase 'Speak for England' (N.B. *not* 'Speak for Britain') was uttered by the Conservative politician Leo Amery to indicate that by hesitating to declare war on Germany following the invasion of Poland in September 1939 the then Prime Minister Neville Chamberlain was failing to 'speak for England'. It was by all accounts a telling intervention, and it was Amery who some months later delivered the death blow to Chamberlain's premiership in the debate over military failure in Norway. He quoted Oliver Cromwell's words to the Long Parliament: 'You have sat too long here for any good you have been doing. Depart, I say, and let us have done with you. In the name of God, go!' The last phrase is regularly parroted by less eloquent Members of Parliament to this day.

How complex 'England' can prove to be is suggested by the fact that the intensely patriotic and imperialist Amery, opposed to appeasement of Hitler in the 1930s but favouring an alliance with Italy, was himself partly of Hungarian Jewish background and was the father of two notorious sons. One, John Amery, was hanged for treason at the end of the Second World War because of his active collaboration with the Nazis, including efforts to establish an English SS unit, the British Free Korps. The second was Julian, an equally colourful figure, who served with the SOE in wartime Yugoslavia and later became a Conservative minister. We seem to be a long way from poetry, but be assured we shall come to it: in England, of course, all roads lead to poetry.

Heinrich Heine wrote in *Religion and Philosophy in Germany*: 'As soon as a religion seeks help from philosophy, its doom is inevitable. Trying to defend itself it talks itself further and further into perdition. Like any other absolutism, religion must not defend itself.'[1] The same may hold true of ideas of nationality and national identity. I'm setting aside the issue of Britishness, which seem to divide rather than unite the population of the British Isles, in order to think about the equally intransigent topic of Englishness, with which Britishness is of course sometimes conflated. Heine also wrote that 'Christianity is an idea, and as such indestructible and immortal, like every idea. But what *is* this idea?'[2] I would like to replace the word 'Christianity' with the word 'Englishness' here. And what is this idea, this Englishness? John of Gaunt's great deathbed speech in *Richard II* – goes disregarded or uncomprehended by the self-absorbed king, who thinks, with one of his later European fellow-monarchs, 'l'état, c'est moi.' Perhaps, though, he follows the grammatical shape of the old man's evocation:

Methinks I am a prophet new inspir'd,
And thus expiring do foretell of him:
His rash fierce blaze of riot cannot last,
For violent fires soon burn out themselves;
Small showers last long, but sudden storms are short;
He tires betimes that spurs too fast betimes;
With eager feeding food doth choke the feeder;
Light vanity, insatiate cormorant,
Consuming means, soon preys upon itself.
This royal throne of kings, this scepter'd isle,
This earth of majesty, this seat of Mars,
This other Eden, demi-paradise,
This fortress built by Nature for herself
Against infection and the hand of war,
This happy breed of men, this little world,
This precious stone set in the silver sea,
Which serves it in the office of a wall,
Or as a moat defensive to a house,
Against the envy of less happier lands;
This blessed plot, this earth, this realm, this England,
This nurse, this teeming womb of royal kings,
Fear'd by their breed, and famous by their birth,
Renowned for their deeds as far from home,
For Christian service and true chivalry,
As is the sepulchre in stubborn Jewry
Of the world's ransom, blessed Mary's Son;
This land of such dear souls, this dear dear land,
Dear for her reputation through the world,
Is now leas'd out – I die pronouncing it –
Like to a tenement or pelting farm.
England, bound in with the triumphant sea,
Whose rocky shore beats back the envious siege
Of wat'ry Neptune, is now bound in with shame,
With inky blots and rotten parchment bonds;
That England, that was wont to conquer others,
Hath made a shameful conquest of itself.
Ah, would the scandal vanish with my life,
How happy then were my ensuing death![3]

In the sentence stretching from 'This royal throne of kings', the main verb is delayed for twenty lines. Clearly this intensifies the rhetorical impact, as image piles on image and we await the resolution, but it also leaves the evocation suspended without a governing tense, making 'this England' a visionary state located neither in past, present nor future. Imaginatively this is a powerful position – that of the timeless, the immanent, the imminent, the possible – but in crudely political terms it is to the same extent vulnerable. It does not require proof, and it cannot supply any.

Qualities attributed to Englishness by politicians and others include democratic institutions, equality before the law, tolerance, sympathy for the underdog, fair play et cetera (Betjeman adds class distinction and proper drains). Depending on the national mood and the state of the economy and how much corruption is in the news this week, these claims may produce a certain amount of hollow laughter; and yet the qualities they refer to are among those we would probably care to be identified with, aspirations to be borne in mind, however remote the possibility of their achievement may seem at any given point, as at the moment. But it is also probable that if the people of England – those who, according to G.K. Chesterton (who was fortunate to predecease local radio and the internet) have 'never spoken yet',[4] were given the opportunity to decide, we should have capital punishment, closed borders, higher wages, lower taxes, an improved NHS funded by moonbeams, no arts funding, and withdrawal from the EU. It begs the question of how *useful* an idea Englishness actually is. It might be truer to describe it as inescapable, like envy or the weather.

If there is always a mismatch between the desiderata and the day-to-day, there is also a tendency for notions of Englishness to sit more readily on the Right than the Left: it is a persistent tendency in Conservatism to view itself and Englishness as effectively synonymous, so that the one supplies the other's credentials and vice versa. It is to this end of the spectrum that a "platonic" England, a perfect original, permanently true and unchanging, also seems to belong. Its adherents can evince the Christianised class tribalism that once defined the Church of

England as 'the Conservative Party at prayer'. This end of the English spectrum may consider itself authentic and original, but it doesn't mind borrowing – 'Jerusalem', for example (William Blake may have been mad but he was no Tory) or the evocative passage from Orwell about spinsters cycling to Mass which was enlisted by the Conservative Prime Minister John Major as one of a number of recent doomed attempts to get hold of the idea of Englishness.

The symbolic capital of the Conservative tribe, its founding tradition, is rural and agricultural, however it has replenished or diminished itself by later involvement in industry and finance, and it is striking that the various myths I shall try briefly to evoke here all show an attachment to the "the country" as a guarantor of authenticity and, in a sense, of originality. A titled lady, on hearing that Labour had won the 1945 general election, declared, 'But the country won't stand for it.' This is, you might say, the political form of the literary mode known as the Pastoral. The myths also involve an interesting circularity in that the rural world, governed by the seasons, is often also felt to be 'timeless'.

One thing that stands at the centre of the vexatious subject of England and Englishness is, of course, language. Its public uses are often, to put it mildly, impure. Repetition and distortion empty it of meaning. Few of those who use it for public purposes have any interest in or even any sense of language as something more than merely instrumental. 'Language? Our Shakespeares will do that for us.' Its aesthetic dimension is of little concern to them: at best it falls into the category of All Very Well – nice but inessential, like art, like culture – and if there is one word that has suffered terribly at the hands of ignorance and laziness lately, it is that word: culture. It will, we know, recover, with time, patience and perhaps a moratorium on its use. Ten years might do. I might place a modest bet with Paddy Power that after the 2012 Olympics we shall hear less of it.

I labour this introduction in order to suggest the kind of madly entangled briar patch into which the subject of Englishness seems to lead us, and to lead to the questions that animate these lectures. Within 'culture', what do poets make of Englishness? What do they mean by it? Can they 'speak for England'? Where is it? When is it or was it or will it be? Can it accommodate change and survive the apparent transfer of authority to Irish and Scots writers and other Anglophone writers further afield? Has it been left behind? Will it be abandoned? Must it be? Is it like the fossil in Peter Porter's poem that 'ascends through slime / To selfhood and in dying finds a face'?[5] Or is there life in the old dog yet? With these things in mind, I want to sketch ideas of England as they manifest themselves in the poets who were most important to me in the years when I was beginning to write, and others who came close on their heels.

Ted Hughes's poem 'Pike' describes fishing at night for an ancient pike in a pond 'as deep as England'.[6] As a fourteen year old I found this a phrase of exciting resonance. Forty-odd years later I would say that the phrase works by identifying time with place, treating them interchangeably to reinforce each other's authority. And I would suggest that the whole mythological project of England works in the same way, whether in the clichés of the heritage industry or in the more exacting sphere of poetry. Shortly after I got to know Hughes's 'Pike' I read a comment by the poet-critic David Holbrook which dismissed that opening phrase – 'It was as deep as England' – as an English equivalent of Welsh *hwyl*, by which he seems to have meant high-flown speech without substance, though that is not how it is defined in Welsh. This seemed rude not only to Hughes but to the Welsh, and I have always instinctively resisted Holbrook's judgement.

As I began in my teens to develop an interior map of poetry (note the metaphor) this merger of place and time took on special prominence. To someone of my age, the indisputably great modern poet presented by the authorities (most notably Mr Grayson, my English teacher) was T.S. Eliot, an American who wanted to be English. After his conversion to Anglicanism, Eliot wrote insistently of the identical facts of place and time. Three of the *Four Quartets* take their titles from English place-names: 'Burnt Norton', 'East Coker' and 'Little Gidding'. (The fourth, 'The Dry Salvages', refers to a group of rocks off the

Massachusetts coast, was once described by the English poet-critic Donald Davie as a parody.) East Coker, in Somerset, is currently under threat from a housing development. Some poets, though probably not Eliot, would think of this as the latest incarnation of the English curse of enclosure, although the place's defenders seem to see it in terms of 'Heritage', which to some observers may seem like the 'soft power' version of the same problem. All his English places were for Eliot sites of faith, of durable meaning, where, as he wrote, 'History is now and England'.[7] The transience of political concerns was trumped by the fact that what he found in his chosen places was, he felt sure, true.

His major successor, W.H. Auden, was also drawn to the imaginative authority with which an older world seemed charged. In his case it was a Norse saga-world which he situated in a country of his own devising, based in the lead-mining country of the North Pennines. Here the machinery of industry, whose very names seemed charged with religious significance, led backwards rather than forward. By the time Auden discovered the mines, they were already in decline, as though relics of the world of feuds and revenge about which he wrote in his early play, *Paid on Both Sides*. Limestone and the waters that ran through it and beneath it seemed like a kind of guarantee on which an imaginative reality could be founded; and that folk-loric world of saga and ballad gave access to certain mysteries which only the poet or the poem could properly enter. These form the ur-world of Auden's poems, and their very language is presented as existing at a level prior to or beyond rational interpretation.

In his book on the fundamentals of prosody, describing the intensified, ritualised attention produced by its organisation into lines, Alfred Corn writes: 'poetry has never fully disengaged itself from its associations with shamanism; the poet, like the shaman, has mastered certain techniques – rhythmic, perform-ative, imagistic, metaphoric – that summon the unconscious part of the mind, so that, in this dreamlike state between waking and sleeping, we may discover more about our thoughts and feelings than we would otherwise be able to do'.[8] Even at his most seemingly rational-analytical, Auden is also serving a shamanic function, and the strongest truth-claims may in fact emerge from this necessarily occluded sphere. 'O where are you going?' is one of the most memorable and least self-explanatory of the early poems:

'O where are you going?' said reader to rider,
'That valley is fatal where furnaces burn,
Yonder's the midden whose odours will madden,
The gap is the grave where the tall return.'
[...]

'Out of this house' – said rider to reader,
'Yours never will' – said farer to fearer,
'They're looking for you' – said hearer to horror,
As he left them there, as he left them there.[9]

John Fuller, in his invaluable *Commentary* on Auden, provides a convincing psychosexual decoding of this early (1931) poem but such analysis cannot help but seem reductive, because it must neglect the dramatising function of the poem's prosody – a ballad form subjected to heavy alliteration and other internal echoes, with simultaneous recurrence and variation of form and phrasing producing the effect of both repetition and instability, most notably in the final stanza, which both abandons the interrogative (change of form apparently indicating resolution) and refuses to answer the questions. The critic may read the poem as a disguise and seek to unmask its wearer, but poetically the disguise is the outcome, the *event*. The *event* of the poem, in which prosody is dominant, shows paraphrasable meaning overwhelmed by crisis (something which reaches an extreme development in the poems of James Fenton, who at one time seemed to be Auden's possible successor).

Auden's myth, like Eliot's, makes claims on history; and like Eliot's it also grants a kind of immunity from human time. A less intellectually ambitious poet, Philip Larkin, wrote of the same Pennine landscape as Auden in 'Show Saturday'. In Larkin's poem, actually based on Bellingham Show in Northumberland, he notes that this public rural affirmation of skills and crafts and community is barely a day's length. Rather like the old high street butchers' and bakers' shops that always seemed no sooner to have opened than to be preparing to close, the showground crowd is soon on its way home. From halfway through the fourth of eight eight-line stanzas the end is taking place, as the horse-boxes, 'like shifting scenery', slowly make their way:

> Back now to private addresses, gates and lamps
> In high stone one-street villages, empty at dusk,
> And side roads of small towns (sports finals stuck
> In front doors, allotments reaching down to the railway);
> Back now to autumn, leaving the ended husk
> Of summer that brought them here for Show Saturday –
> [...]

> Back now, all of them, to their local lives:
> [...]

> To winter coming, as the dismantled Show
> Itself dies back into the area of work.
> Let it stay hidden there like strength, below
> Sale-bills and swindling; something people do,
> Not noticing how time's rolling smithy-smoke
> Shadows much greater gestures; something they share
> That breaks ancestrally each year into
> Regenerate union. Let it always be there.[10]

Englishness in poetry, it goes almost without saying, is often elegiac, its affirmations at their most powerful at the point of leavetaking. It may even have a death-wish secretly and pre-emptively inscribed within it. No sympathy with Larkin's politics is required to be moved by the extraordinarily vivid evocation mustered in 'Show Saturday', so much more powerful than anything Betjeman could muster. 'Let it always be there,' Larkin ends. Yet compare the much inferior 'Going, Going', a rather muzzily unfocussed protest against the perceived decline of the country into greed and vulgarity and ignorance, where Larkin fears that 'that will be England gone'.[11] Perhaps it would be true to say that for good and/or ill, it would be a *version* of England gone, a constellation of fetish-objects whose natural home is the correspondence columns of *The Daily Telegraph* and the irascible symposia of saloon bar philosopher-kings in the Home Counties. The vision sours when exploited.

Larkin was all too aware of time and mortality. In the absence of the religious convictions of Eliot and Auden, retrospect could never be enough, and anyway he lacked the materials and the required imaginative combination of luck, arrogance and endurance to create a mythology – and yet he is the most imitated poet of the three, and the best loved, which may make him more typical for the audience than the others.

These visions are all fundamentally rural (or even pre-urban). Eliot's visionary moments depend on such a context: for him the city is often a manifestation of Hell. Auden's Pennines are places from which the imagination derives and to which it returns for an image of underlying truth and authority ('What I see is a limestone landscape').[12] Larkin laments a tradition broken, he imagines, by the First World War – 'Never such innocence again'[13] – a conflict which marked the death of the notion of England as inherently or fundamentally rural. Yet the death of the idea did not kill off the attachment to it.

The First World War marked Ted Hughes's imagination very deeply. In one shocking phrase, he wrote that his father had been 'heavily killed'[14] in the war (he had in fact survived but remained terribly damaged). Part of Hughes's response was to immerse himself ever more deeply in the rural, in isolated settings. One of these was the ancient Kingdom of Elmet, mysteriously situated anywhere from the borders of East Yorkshire to Halifax in the far west of the county. Its core, around Mytholmroyd and Hebden Bridge, is a zone where industry is seen, perhaps gratifyingly, declining into the earth from which it arose around the rivers of the Pennines. Political history has vanished entirely in Hughes's account. He also invested his imagination and his agricultural labour in the secretive valleys of Devon.

From these attachments in Hughes there emerges a fundamental dualism – on the one hand "the natural", on the other a preoccupation with violence which is both "natural" and at some level relishable. This blend is a kind of sophisticated atavism, the atavism of a poet who was as much a bookman as a naturalist. It's interesting in this respect to compare Hughes with a poet with a great deal more apparent warrant for an attachment to violence, his friend and collaborator Seamus Heaney, who laments the drowning of kittens and in sorrow and horror counts the cost of the violence done by people against other people. (The First World War is of course as powerfully remembered in the North of Ireland as in the North of England.) Born in 1930, Hughes, as for various reasons did Larkin (unfit) and Auden (in the USA) and Eliot (too old) before him, missed both world wars, but his imagination is a battlefield, where thistles are mown down as in 'a feud' and are then seen 'stiff with weapons, fighting back over the same ground'.[15] Hughes also identified what he saw as the psychopathic Viking belligerence lightly submerged in the minds of Yorkshiremen, and as any Yorkshireman would tell you, Yorkshire is in fact really England, only better, and any doubts about this can be addressed in the car park.

In his later years, as Poet Laureate, serving as poacher turned gamekeeper and as would-be national myth-maker (sometimes to the baffled scorn of the press) Hughes wrote of a distinction between historical time and the real, presiding extra-historical Time embodied in the person of the Queen Mother, which seems a grotesquely large amount of authority to exert on one very small person. This has the convenient effect – from a royalist point of view – of making politics irrelevant, though where it leaves the First World War is anybody's guess. But we don't of course look to poets primarily for logical constructions. They are imaginative rhetoricians, able, or at any rate often attempting, to bind or inhabit contradiction.

If it was possible to see Eliot, Auden and Hughes as, however variously, parts of the same enterprise, two of Hughes's contemporaries served to complicate matters. These were two Midlanders, raised in or near the fiery core of the Industrial Revolution. On the one hand we have Geoffrey Hill (*b.* 1932), much of whose work seems oddly untouched by the city next door to his native Bromsgove, as was that of an earlier Bromsgrovian, A.E.Housman. On the other, we have Roy Fisher (*b.* 1930) from Handsworth in the heart of Birmingham, who has written voluminously about the city he describes as 'what I think with'.[16]

In a dispute some years ago in the *London Review of Books*, Craig Raine took issue with Tom Paulin over Paulin's dismissal of Hill, claiming that there was something inherently English in Hill's work that Paulin, an Ulsterman and a republican socialist (actually born in York) was incapable of apprehending. At times, though, and not just to Paulin but to other unlucky members of 'lesser tribes without the law', the essentialist English Hill might seem rather like the Cheshire cat, something that becomes invisible as it is looked at – though of course the Cheshire Cat is always smiling, which is not an accusation that can be levelled at Hill. Raine's recourse to essentialism might be seen as an act of critical desperation, an assertion of faith, a drawing of a line beyond which there can be no argument.

In what are perhaps Hill's most famous lines, 'Funeral Music', his series of sonnets about the Wars of the Roses, the death of one England and the birth of another, are focussed at the ferocious battle of Towton, fought in a snowstorm on 29 March 1461, Palm Sunday, the warriors 'livid and featureless, / With England crouched beastwise beneath it all. / "Oh, that old northern business..." ' [17] 28,000 men were at the time reputed to have died in this, the bloodiest battle of the extended civil war which was formally ended in 1485. Towton, interestingly, is near Sherburn-in-Elmet, which in name at least stands on the eastern edge of Hughes's imagined kingdom. It is also a place that visitors find still carries a chill, as of Wordsworth's 'old, unhappy far-off things'.[18] The site of battle itself is a low eminence of fields with no apparent horizons, with a concealed stream where the defeated Lancastrians were trapped and put to the sword by their Yorkist pursuers in a slaughter viewed as exceptional for the times, a fight to the finish where it was agreed in advance that there would be no quarter. The field of Towton is a landscape which seems both representative of 'an idea of England', yet also, in its pitiless massiveness, more like 'the vasty fields' of northern and central France, to which many of the participants were ancestrally connected, than familiar images of rural England. As we seem somehow to be approaching deepest England, with its ancient strife and savagery, we find ourselves simultaneously in 'la France profonde'. This is a connection scarcely to be admitted in public in England at present, when Francophobia seems, to those who voice it, more than ever self-evidently justified. But it's there, nevertheless. And rather than a single England, there may be Englands, like the 'Englands of the Mind' that Seamus Heaney wrote about in a famous essay on Hughes, Larkin and Hill, imagined places overlapping like a Venn diagram. And these Englands seek out their aptest forms in poetry.

While the work which made Hill famous is always conspicuously made, ceremoniously and brilliantly *achieved*, Roy Fisher writes an endlessly adaptable free verse, as if – paradoxically, given his work's Birmingham birthplace – it were the opposite of mass manufacture. Fisher's poems are often intensely seen yet rarely in a straightforward sense representational, and he delivers the following crisp and economical *non serviam* before the accumulated weight of English rhetoric:

Because it could do it well
the poem wants to glorify suffering
I distrust it

I mistrust the poem in the hour of its success,
a thing capable of being
tempted into ethics by the wonderful [19]

There is no reason to suppose that Fisher has Hill in mind here, but it is interesting to consider that what Fisher seems to want to do is resist the reification of theme, place, feeling, attitude and conception of history that is always likely to accompany a poetic tradition. Another famous Fisher poem, 'For Realism', re-imagines an ordinary evening in the Midlands in visually empirical yet near-mystical terms, and presents a strange tantalising parallel to the landscape and bloodstained snow of Hill's battlefield, in the vicinity of Lucas's lamp factory as the back shift comes off at 9pm:

Above, dignity. A new precinct
comes over the scraped hill,
flats on the ridge get the last light.

Down Wheeler Street, the lamps
already gone, the windows have

lake stretches of silver
gashed out of tea-green shadows,
the after-images of brickwork.

A conscience
builds, late, on the ridge. A realism
tries to record, before they're gone,
what silver filth these drains have run.[20]

Cf. 'Funeral Music', 3:

They bespoke doomsday and they meant it by
God, their curved metal rimming the low ridge.
[...]

With England crouched beastwise beneath it all
[...]

Among carnage the most delicate souls
Tup in their marriage-blood, gasping 'Jesus'.[21]

On the far side of the sense of suffocation and confinement
and loss of energy which helped lead Pound and Eliot into
modernism stands Fisher's work. Where the founders of poetic
modernism either broke or re-wrote tradition the better to come
at a history which habit and rhetoric had obscured, Fisher
arrives as a poet in the middle of the twentieth century, and
the history that most interests him is the history of the present,
his own immediate world and lifetime, with the Second World
War as perhaps a starting point and very little before it seeming
to find its way into the poems. (Since Fisher's retirement, of
course, he has written evoking more remote periods, in land-
scapes – the western Peak District – which seemingly encourage
him to do so.) A man born amid industry may feel little connec-
tion to the world of before – his own class may have been
swiftly disconnected from it – before Birmingham became the
fiery metropolis of unceasing hammer-blows. Shakespeare's
home landscape may be only a bus-ride away, but as we have
seen, among ideas of England, time and space can manage a
surprising (and sometimes impenetrable) elasticity: the past, as
Michael Donaghy wrote, 'falls open anywhere'.[22] To close with,

a Fisher poem from the mid-sixties seems to draw tantalisingly together various of the themes and attitudes I've referred to. This is 'An English Sensibility', and it ends:

Out in the cokehouse
cobweb
a dark mat
draped on the rubble in a corner
muffled
with a fog of glittering dust
that shakes
captive
in the sunlight
over pitted silver-grey
ghost shapes that shine through.[23]

'Ghost shapes', 'a fog of glittering dust', – sometimes that seems to be what we're trying to get hold of.

Enemies Within

I ended the first lecture in this series with a brief discussion of the work of Geoffrey Hill and Roy Fisher, suggesting that Fisher offered an innovative way of seeing, one which seemed to free him of some of the obligations and assumptions to which English poets can seem subject. Yet, as is often the way, the subsequent generation (or that significant part of it that I want to talk about) did not for the most part turn to Fisher as a practical example, although his work has been widely regarded as exemplary.

The generation which includes Tony Harrison, Douglas Dunn and Jeffrey Wainwright was of a more explicitly political cast of imagination, both in subject-matter and in attitudes to form. I want to start by glancing at these poets' depictions of England, noting at the outset that their Englands are inescapably historical, whether because they write about the past or because the influence of the past is so powerfully felt in the poets' own present tenses.

Whether they formulated it to themselves or not, the question Harrison and Dunn and Wainwright all faced was: how to write the History poem. This poetic category, which I suspect I may be inventing accidentally out of thin air, is occupied by poems which try to take a view of a time, a society, to describe the climate of an era, as distinct from poems whose focus is more proverbial or lyric or local or personal, though all these elements may have a place in the History poem.

A scattered sample of History poems in English would include, for example, Marvell's 'An Horatian Ode upon Cromwell's Return from Ireland', Samuel Johnson's 'The Vanity of Human Wishes', the passages in Wordsworth's *The Prelude* dealing with the French Revolution, Matthew Arnold's 'Dover

Beach', Ezra Pound's 'Mauberley', Yeats's 'Easter 1916', Auden's 'The Fall of Rome', Louis Simpson's 'To the Western World' and perhaps Robert Lowell's 'Waking Early Sunday Morning', as well as work by Harrison, Ken Smith, Dunn and Wainwright.

The desire to write History poems in the generation of English poets born between about 1937 and 1945 (Dunn of course is Scots but has written important work in and about England), has much to do with class, and with the sense that the England represented in the poetry they grew up among seemed partial, and, after the 1930s, depoliticised. Quite how deeply class assumptions were embedded in everyday conscious-ness is illustrated by the response of the one-time 1930s Marxist Stephen Spender to the work of Tony Harrison, a working-class scholarship student from Leeds. Spender described him as 'a changeling',[1] meaning presumably that no one of that background could produce work of such accomplishment and ambition. Now of course we find ourselves living through a period when the aim of the government seems to be to ensure that no more such 'changelings' slip through the net into higher education.

Roy Fisher's patient quarrying of the visible, material environ-ment was one fruitful approach, but the beneficiaries of the 1944 Education Act had, some of them, a more historicised and explicitly radical sense of England, fed by a quarrel with tradition rather than an embrace of transatlantic Modernism. This radicalism was not on offer either from the poets associated with the Movement, who, if they had ground in common – and it seems less the case as time goes on – tended to balance a cautious reason against an innate pessimism; nor from Ted Hughes, whose interests lay elsewhere ; nor from the now slightly neglected figure of Thom Gunn, whose sense of history was often heroic (see his poem about Claus Von Stauffenberg, leader of the July plot against Hitler in 1944), existential and individualist, its early phase culminating in a vision of a form of tragic hipness perfected in the poem 'My Sad Captains':

True, they are not at rest yet,
but now they are indeed
apart, winnowed from failures,

they withdraw to an orbit
and turn with disinterested
hard energy, like the stars.[2]

This is wonderful, but pinups were not quite what the times, and the generation succeeding Gunn, seemed to require.

One approach would be to write as if England were not its familiar self, but another place, new-made, freshly opened to the imagination. A classic of postwar English poetry is Jeffrey Wainwright's '1815', which visits the year of the Battle of Waterloo in four sections marked out by what at first reading seemed an almost intolerable plainness:

1815

I *The Mill-Girl*

Above her face
Dead roach stare vertically
Out of the canal.
Water fills her ears,
Her nose her open mouth.
Surfacing, her bloodless fingers
Nudge the drying gills.

The graves have not
A foot's width between them.
Apprentices, jiggers, spinners
Fill them straight from work,
Common as smoke.

Waterloo is all the rage;
Coal and iron and wool
Have supplied the English miracle.

II *Another Part of the Field*

The dead on all sides –
The fallen –
The deep-chested rosy ploughboys
Swell out of their uniforms.

The apple trees,
That were dressed overall,
Lie stripped about their heads,

'The French cavalry
Came up very well my lord.'
'Yes. And they went down
Very well too.
Overturned like turtles.
Our muskets were obliged
To their white bellies.'

No flies on Wellington.
His spruce wit sits straight
In the saddle, jogging by.

III *The Important Man*

Bothered by his wife
From a good dinner,
The lock-keeper goes down
To the ponderous water's edge
To steer in the new corpse.

A bargee, shouting to be let through,
Stumps over the bulging lengths
Of his hatches,
Cursing the slowness
Of water.

The lock-keeper bends and pulls her out
With his bare hands.
Her white eyes, rolled upwards,
Just stare.

He is an important man now.
Her turns to his charge:
The water flows uphill.

IV *Death of the Mill-Owner*

Shaking the black earth
From a root of potatoes,
The gardener walks
To the kitchen door.

The trees rattle
Their empty branches together.

Upstairs the old man
Is surprised.
His fat body clenches –
Mortified
At what is happening.[3]

Wainwright makes rhetoric from the seeming absence of rhetoric. Section 1, 'The Mill Girl' begins with a drowned body in a canal and moves in an unannounced way from this one instance to a clipped conclusion: what is it that generates the 'English miracle'? It is war, with industry on a war footing to supply war's voracious hunger. The dead – the drowned girl, the mill-hands moving without a break from workplace to graveyard – are the collateral damage necessary to the miracle's fulfilment. The very absence of authorial comment (combined with the eerie gliding assurance of Wainwright's ear and some laconic punning) delivers this world to us afresh: whatever we thought we knew, it seems we knew nothing. The mill-girl herself cannot help but remind us of Ophelia in *Hamlet*, but this drowned girl is anonymous and has neither mourners nor Gertrude's elegiac description:

There is a willow grows aslant the brook
That shows his hoar leaves in the glassy stream;
Therewith fantastic garlands did she make
Of crowflowers, nettles, daisies, and long purples
That liberal shepherds give a grosser name,
But our cold maids do dead men's fingers call them.
There, on the pendent boughs her coronet weeds
Clamb'ring to hang, an envious sliver broke;
When down her weedy trophies and herself
Fell in the weeping brook. Her clothes spread wide
And, mermaid-like, awhile they bore her up;
Which time she chanted snatches of old lauds,
As one incapable of her own distress,
Or like a creature native and indued
Unto that element; but long it could not be
Till that her garments, heavy with their drink,
Pull'd the poor wretch from her melodious lay
To muddy death.[4]

Perhaps for reasons of her own, Gertrude's speech, describing events she seems not to have witnessed, seems deliberately to poeticise the drowning, to lend beauty to a premature death. Death in Wainwright's poem is presented without adornment, but with a sort of pictorial realism which seems to satirise the painting which comes to many people's minds when hearing Shakespeare's words, namely Millais's 'Ophelia', painted in 1851-52, long after the events described in Wainwright's poem. What many people also know is that Lizzie Siddal, Millais's model, lay fully clothed in a cold bath and nearly caught her death of cold – for which the painter apparently had to pay her father compensation. Presumably no such compensation was considered in the case of the mill girl. In any case, who could say who or where her parents are, or were, among thousands of such people forced into the mills by economic change? Ranging back and forth across history, Wainwright makes it impossible to consider it done with, another part of 'that old Northern business'.

In '1815' Ophelia's 'brook' has become a canal, an industrial artery. Four times Wainwright goes to this well of history. Four times he refuses what might to most of us seem the irresistible opportunity to comment, to judge, to write the kind of political poetry which often tends to make English readers uneasy and suspicious that they are being instructed. It is much harder to mount a defence against Wainwright's vision: this, you come to imagine, is what England amounted to and what it has been declining from ever since and trying with varying success, as now, to recapture: this pitiless strangeness, this England on which "heritage" will never manage to lay a condescending hand.

In fact '1815' is an elegy of sorts, for the pastoral tradition of poetry which is the poem's parent. The anonymous dead – the mill-girl, the plough-boys – are figures displaced from the secondary world of pastoral, a world rich in convention, proof against time even though time is a major subject of pastoral, and forced into the "real" world beloved of business, finance and Human Resources, a place in which, Marx and Engels point out, 'all that is solid melts into air'.[5] The pastoral is the creation of economic and hereditary powers whose interests have, by the period of Wainwright's poem, encountered serious challenges and in many cases are adapting and moving on.

Where Andrew Marvell, in 'Upon Appleton House' wrote of the civilised retirement of the Parliamentarian general Sir Thomas Fairfax to his estate in East Yorkshire, in Wainwright's poem we see Wellington touring the battlefield at Waterloo, sang-froid intact among the carnage. Wellington's comments ever-so-faintly echo Marvell's 'Bermudas'. Wellington compares the white uniforms of the French infantry to the white bellies of turtles, whereas Marvell has canoes carried upside down in the heads of their oarsmen. The supine dead and the inverted boats are both glimpses of 'a world turned upside down'. The 1643 broadside ballad of that name, which laments the Puritan insistence that Christmas be a solemn religious feast rather than a time of pleasure, the lyric offers a shadowy foretelling of the world depicted in '1815':

> Command is given, we must obey, and quite forget old Christmas day:
> Kill a thousand men, or a Town regain, we will give thanks and praise amain.
> The wine pot shall clinke, we will feast and drinke.
> And then strange motions will abound.
> Yet let's be content, and the times lament, you see the world turn'd upside down.
>
> Our Lords and Knights, and Gentry too, doe mean old fashions to forgoe:
> They set a porter at the gate, that none must enter in thereat.
> They count it a sin, when poor people come in.
> Hospitality it selfe is drown'd.
> Yet let's be content, and the times lament, you see the world turn'd upside down.

The porter at the gate might metamorphose into the lock-keeper, for the canal is someone's estate, while the estate of the poor is early death. The death of the mill-owner in the final part of the poem – a peremptory announcement, not a lament (we recall that the mill-girl likewise went unlamented) – evokes another poem from the Civil War period, James Shirley's 'The glories of our blood and state', often known as 'Death the Leveller', originally a song from his play *The Contention of Ajax and Ulysses for the Armour of Achilles*:

The glories of our blood and state,
    Are shadows, not substantial things,
There is no armour against fate,
    Death lays his icy hand on Kings,
        Sceptre and Crown,
        Must tumble down,
And in the dust be equal made,
With the poor crooked scithe and spade.

Some men with swords may reap the field,
    And plant fresh laurels where they kill,
But their strong nerves at last must yield,
    They tame but one another still;
        Early or late,
        They stoop to fate,
And must give up their murmuring breath,
When they pale Captives creep to death.

The Garlands wither on your brow,
    Then boast no more your mighty deeds,
Upon Deaths purple Altar now
    See where the Victor-victim bleeds,
        Your heads must come,
        To the cold Tomb,
Onely the actions of the just
Smell sweet, and blossom in their dust.

One way in which we might interpret this haunting poem in our time is suggested by Roger McGough's comic recasting of it in 'Streemin', spoken by a pupil consigned to the bottom stream in school: 'all this divishns / arent reely fair. / look at the cemtery − / no streemin there.'[6] But it is said that King Charles II liked Shirley's poem, presumably having a rather different interpretation of it. Meanwhile, in Wainwright's poem, the death of the mill-owner is merely a fact: in itself it alters nothing, but the world alters around it, and the water of the canal has been persuaded to run uphill through the locks − a revolution itself soon to be superseded by the railways. Among the myth-makers, Wainwright creates an anti-myth, the world shown as though without origins.

The fundamental insecurity of English life is the only consistent thing, in Wainwright's vision. The 'poor pelting villages'[7] of *King Lear* and the 'pelting farms'[8] of *Richard II* give place to industrial graveyards and a 'realism' about the economic basis of human affairs that in our own time we seem to be revisiting – revisiting with a sudden force which leaves many feeling that it is not only their livelihoods but their identities which are under threat, when 'man is a wolf to man'[9] and dispossession becomes rational and necessary in the minds of the dispossessors.

I anticipate part of my third lecture here, but in the poetry written now these conditions rarely figure in a direct sense: disquiet, where it appears, does so half-covertly, it seems, as in the rurally-focused work of Jacob Polley – or in *Edgelands*, the prose collaboration between Paul Farley and Michael Symmons Roberts, which rejects what it sees as the nihilism of some psychogeography in favour of the power of reclamation and adaptation. But to return: the fate of Wainwright's dead mill-girl and the innumerable dead factory hands find their contemporary equivalent less in the work of poets than in the world depicted by a novelist, in Ross Raisin's recent novel *Waterline*. In it a former worker in the Clydeside shipyards becomes a widower, undergoes a breakdown and becomes homeless. Drawn to London, he finds temporary work in an airport hotel, but when the staff try to unionise he is made redundant and descends into destitution and alcoholism. His powerlessness to gain a purchase on his own life recalls figures such as Wordsworth's beggar-woman, who has travelled to America and back in vain hope of sustenance. Dispossession is as much 'an idea of England' as pastoral tranquillity. In the present day, Larkin wrote, 'no one actually starves',[10] but none the less the distribution of food parcels to families some of which are in work is a sign of the times which binds us to the dispossessed of '1815'.

E.P. Thompson wrote that the English working class was present at its own birth: Wainwright shows that class as though at a pre-conscious moment. Across the Pennines from Wainwright's Manchester Cottonopolis, Tony Harrison, from Leeds, also imagined an early stage of the Industrial Revolution among the machine-breakers when the authorities feared insurrection of the kind that had recently been seen across the English Channel.

Harrison's work is intensely sensuous and realised, but it's striking how at times he devotes comparatively little interest to the visible, compared with Wainwright's poem. It is the texture of language itself, and the power it confers, and the restraints under which some of its users labour, that most concern him: 'the tongueless man gets his land took',[11] remarks one of the voices which passes through his poems. Not all language is equal, it seems, and to be 'a Bad Hand at Righting'[12] is, or was, possibly a fatal disadvantage, while accent itself is shown as a sort of doom, if you have a non-standard accent. Harrison's revenge on the English teacher who would not allow him to read Keats aloud is famous, as is the teacher's later apologetic purchase of one of Harrison's books, which he asked the author to sign. To a certain way of thinking, such problems are "historical", "over" and, in effect, no longer problematic, but in a broader sense the silence of the linguistic underclass illuminates a more general point about language – that the owners of language still use it as a means of discrimination, not among shades of meaning but among classes, and that the linguistic dispossessed feel no secure claim on language when it is both reified by the powerful and mysteriously inaccessible to the powerless who don't know the rules of the game. Linguistic confidence and a standard accent will take you to a lot of places – a Russell Group university, for example.

Learning to play the game, or to change the rules, has its own penalties too. Over and again Harrison returns to the paradox whereby articulacy – which is both the power and affliction of the vengeful scholarship boy – separates its possessor from his class and his origins. Harrison also introduces a complicating sense that the working class has not been in all times and places fissionable material awaiting a revolutionary spark, but might prove just as likely – as in the case of the poets' parents – to endure patiently and hope for not very much at all, caught in the pre-political condition of having no stake in history and no leverage on it. Another observer of these conditions, Douglas Dunn, wrote: 'You hardly notice you have grown too old to cry out for change.'[13] There is a bitter bareness and monochrome chill to Harrison's sense of the domestic world of his upbringing, as well as the sense of completeness that often accompanies myth.

Perhaps the immediate contemporary equivalent is found not

so much in material want (though this is increasingly apparent once more) but in the occasional nightmarish sense that people no longer consider themselves to be using language, feeling perhaps that the world is elsewhere and that language is simply the token that would gain you admission. These may, of course, simply be the complaints of someone of sixty-odd, though that wouldn't necessarily make them untrue. Where Harrison, a Classicist by training, a dramatist who stages his work in Greece and draws on Greek tragedy, depicts the dilemmas which echo the work of Aeschylus and Sophocles, his lineal successor – yet to emerge, it seems – might turn for another look at Euripides's *The Bacchae*. Who is actually funding the visit of the offended god Dionysos to our city? The Bilderberg Group? And to what end?

In a sense the sonnets from Harrison's *The School of Eloquence* are so familiar now that for the moment we are hardly able to read them: for many readers they have become the very climate in which the imagining of history takes place. Yet their concern to pursue a dialectic of the relation between privileged forms – the sonnet, the iambic line – and the urge to speak out of 'the silence round all poetry'[14] is genuinely radical. Readers of Harrison's work may come to feel the same chill, the sense that truly we are unaccommodated in the world, which arises from Wainwright's very different work. Where is it we live? And, as the football crowds chant, 'Who are yer?'

I suggested that Harrison is not primarily a poet of the visible. Yet he is a playwright and an innovative film-maker, and his poems reveal a love of the cinema, James Cagney in particular, as well as erotic scenes involving the sharing of cigarettes between lovers. *Prometheus*, his 1998 feature film, has substantial passages set in a cinema near the cooling towers at Ferrybridge, where the actor Walter Sparrow sits in the stalls smoking and watching people smoke. Ultimately the cinema burns down, marking a triumph of ignorant power over Sparrow's innocent but seemingly outmoded 'culture of consolation'.

The visible world seems to function for Harrison as a complement to language, perhaps a sort of counter-melody of light. It was, of course, a film that got Harrison into trouble, the poem-film v., set in a graveyard in Leeds during the 1984-85 miners' strike. It was the language what did it, guv, the relentlessly casual foul-mouthedness of the skinhead who debates with the narrator, but had the poem remained on the page it is unlikely that there would have been any fuss at all. Tory backbenchers don't normally find themselves reading poems, or even noticing their existence, any more than journalists on the *Mail* or the *Express*. Strangely, there seems to have been no fuss at all about Richard Curtis's 'adaptation' from Shakespeare, 'The Skinhead Hamlet' ('fuck off to a nunnery'; 'fuck me, I'm fucked' [15] etc) which remained safely on the silent page. Given the profanity available on television every night nowadays, it's hard to see how there could have been such a fuss about Harrison's v. even a generation ago. What is more interesting is that the uproar occurred at the very point when, as Terry Eagleton pointed out, Harrison began to sound like a liberal rather than a radical poet. England, by the account offered in v. is a house divided, rather than, as seemed particularly evident at the time of composition, a collection of tribes bound by mutual hatred and contempt.

Harrison's determination to take possession of the forms of literary privilege was likewise a concern for Douglas Dunn in *Barbarians*. A good deal of this 1979 collection is set in England, including the grimly brilliant counter-factual poem 'Gardeners', set in Loamshire in 1789, where the workers on a great rural estate stage a revolt:

Townsmen will wonder, when your house was burned,
We did not burn your gardens and undo
What likes of us did for the likes of you;
We did not raze this garden that we made,
Although we hanged you somewhere in its shade.[16]

In the work of a poem born slightly later, the late Peter Reading, news of whose death emerged while this lecture was being written, such a vision is countered with a complicating response to the idea of the collective. Reading's work does many things. One of them is to manifest how liberal exhaustion may breed intolerance out of despair. If Reading was ever a socialist, you might infer that he came to view Socialism as too good for people. Whether through principle or convenience, many people who have tried to enact it have come to feel the same way,

A poet of enormous invention and ingenuity, sometimes writing at book-length and often designing the typography and layout of the work himself, Reading used classical forms while painting a Swiftian picture of a nightmarish society whose fundamental division is not economic but intellectual and moral. Behind this grotesque creation, this tabloid, crapulous country of the tiny mind, lies the counter-example of Reading's predecessor as Shropshire poet, his fellow-Classicist A.E. Housman. Housman's pessimism is framed in terms of an England next door to England, where a classical world of athletes, drink and early death bleeds into an English rural equivalent, its date carefully imprecise, its laws somewhat akin to Hardy's in their reliably fatal severity. Shropshire lads, Ludlow jail, beer, early death as much desired as feared – this blend has taken a powerful and unyielding grip on the English imagination, perhaps because of the force of its appeal to what A.S. Byatt calls 'the English feeling', a sense of the omnipresent familiarity of death. It is hard to characterise such a huge body of work as Reading's – three volumes of *Collected Poems* and two final collections – but one element involves Reading's reversing the poles of Housman's work so that instead of rural life taking on the tragic dignity of classical attitudes and form, tragedy is travestied by its circumstances, as in the third part of 'Duologues':

'I wish I'd knowed im as drives tractor, afore I wed Jim.
Once you marries the wrong un youm never the same someow.'

'Same along o me, Annie, that un as I fancied first,
e never said much all them years as us was courtin,
so I thinks as e dunna like me, an breaks up with im.
Then e thinks as I dunna like im, an takes some wench else.
Then I sid im again, one Pig Day it were in the Arms,
and e says as e loves me an would I get wed to im
(only would I answer im quick or eed af to wed er).
Well, I never says "ar" nor "no" for days, till e thinks
as it's "no" and e weds this other out Clungunford way
an they moves down Tenbury country – Glebe Farm an summat.
An e dunna get on with er, an just now e writes me

as e loves me, an I writes back as I loves im an all.
Just now all is stock dies – that Foot and Mouth year afore last –
and they says as e got debts an that's why e shot isself.' [17]

This is the collapsed star of the pastoral tradition, with the second speaker as Marvell's Juliana, who first steals the Mower's reason and then kills him off. So much for 'the silence round all poetry'. The effect, in the larger context of Reading's work, is to suggest that the consolations of a personal myth have become unavailable, even supposing the instinct to create one had survived. Ranged against Reading and the admired dead and a few likeminded contemporaries, is a population which seems to consist almost entirely of morons – vandals, thugs, headline writers, ignorant members of the provincial bourgeoisie ('What do you write about then, Pete?' 'Cunts like you, mate'),[18] manglers of language, destroyers of the environment.

Reading's approach is often to use ignorance against itself by allowing it to speak in its own words. After beginning as a faintly Romantic pessimist (a strain which resurfaced occasionally at a later date) he began to empty his own language of metaphor and image: in contrast to the dandified richness of contemporaries such as Craig Raine and Christopher Reid, his work becomes a poetry of statement whose memorability derives from a combination of moral force and formal assurance. The reader looking for a way to sustain and unify egalitarian politics and poetic art receives only limited encouragement from Reading, whose gaze is increasingly directed beyond "society" towards a vision of geological historical vastness where species decline is inescapable and the best thing to do is watch birds and stay drunk.

To use a grotesque analogy, in comparison with Wainwright and Harrison, Reading seems as the Earl of Rochester might have done to the Metaphysicals, an energetic nihilist whose pessimism led him to a brutal and inescapable conclusion. In the words of Private Frazer, 'We're doomed. Aye, we're doomed.' To a Marxist it might look like bourgeois individualism, albeit on the rim of the volcano, but in another sense Reading may simply be arriving early at the state of political exhaustion that can be found, explicitly or implicitly, in a good deal of contemporary poetry which is still enjoying a post-Ashbery narcosis, in some cases state-maintained (but watch out), in which things, like, happen and, like, don't add up.

One other poet who might have arrived at a myth is James Fenton, but his best poem, 'A Staffordshire Murderer', seems to mark the end of a line of development rather than the beginning – to the frustration of some readers. Fenton's great master is Auden, and it is striking that 'A Staffordshire Murderer' comes close to loss or abandonment of coherence, or of comprehensibility, as Auden's 'O where are you going' also does. Indeed, incomprehensibility is part of the poem's subject. It seems there is a barrier beyond which there might lie an understanding which it may not be in poetry's interests to share with us:

> Every fear is a desire. Every desire is a fear.
> The cigarettes are burning under the tree
> Where the Staffordshire murderers wait for their accomplices
> And victims. Every victim is an accomplice.[19]

It is never clear in Fenton's poem who the narrator is – murderer, poet, observer, accomplice. Meanwhile 'we hear nothing, / Or what we hear we do not understand'.[20] We seem to have trespassed on the other side of the mirror, where we can recognise threats and warnings but not their specific reference or import. In this England it makes perfect sense for Stafford-shire to have its murderer (a series exists in Staffordshire pottery) just as in songs Lancashire has its soldier or Lincolnshire its poacher – or Yorkshire its Ripper. Blake Morrison wrote an extended poem, 'The Ballad of the Yorkshire Ripper', that tried in part to grasp how Peter Sutcliffe was as much a product of history and biology as anyone else. But so far it has been left to a novelist, David Peace, to investigate more fully the mythological possibilities of that subject, in his *Red Riding* series of novels. Here a corrupted murder investigation exercises a fatal attraction for those who would set it right. Nightmares of guilt and terror find an exact equivalent in the landscapes of West Yorkshire, while the mad wing of the almost-supernatural can be heard beating somewhere nearby. Interestingly, Peace's novel of the miners' strike, *GB84*, partakes of the same eerie climate while dealing with an intransigently "material" subject.

Knowingly or not, the intensity of mood, rhetorical insistence and repetition which dominate David Peace's writing are, I would suggest, efforts to cross over into poetry, for this – murder, guilt, sacrifice, atonement and the self-interest of power – is a subject whose true setting must be the poem, the most ritualistic of literary forms, the home of myth. But no one has successfully done this to date.

Why not? Perhaps in part because of a lack of faith on the part of poets in the viability of sustained narrative. But crime, the crime novel, true crime, the crime drama, the highly publicised and atrocious real-life crime, especially the kind that insists on the connection between sex and death, is perhaps *the* English subject of the present day. Auden wrote a famous essay called 'The Guilty Vicarage', where he set out a view of detective novels as rituals concerning the restoration of an order which crime has disrupted. Clues are markers on the detective's journey. Nowadays, of course, it is less likely that the landscape would be scattered with polite hints – books of matches from the Blue Monkey club, railway tickets to Basingstoke – than with body parts. The English, as Orwell pointed out, have always liked a good murder, as have people of all nations, but the extremity and atrocity depicted in much contemporary crime fiction in England possesses, albeit unintentionally, a political dimension in that it involves the un-writing of history. To choose only two prominent examples, the work of writers such as Val McDermid (a Scot who writes about the North of England) and Mo Hayder, whose work is set around Bristol, is necessarily to some degree concerned with motives and causes, but these are ultimately means of staging the dreadful act which fascinates even as it defeats comprehension. (As with Agatha Christie, motive is only a necessary formal pretext for the murder, a reason for forensic rather than moral investigation.) The usual rationale for the extreme, graphic depiction of violence is that the world itself is a violent place and that the author is obliged to reflect existing conditions. But there is something disingenuous or perhaps naïve here: is there nothing to be left to the imagination, as it was on the Greek tragic stage? One effect of extremity as currently depicted is to diminish the role of cause; there is no sense in such work that 'to understand all is to forgive all'. We have disposed of God; at the same time we have reinstated the idea of evil in the form of something inexplicable and inhuman which in a sense sanctifies the impulse towards revenge. The book's solved crime is a form of rhetorical revenge on behalf of the community: whether the villain dies or not, the end of the book is a symbolic public execution in which vengeance trumps mere history made up of causes and effects. In this sense, crime writing, in its predominantly reactionary form (it does take other forms at times) is particularly well-adapted to the impatient, intolerant, mood so often encountered in contemporary England – a strange mixture of brutality and sentimentality, whose preoccupations feel tangible as economics, even now, does not.

England, as poets have often shown, is a fertile killing-ground. The public hunger for the Danish crime series *The Killing* arises partly because we know that its turf is really ours, just as Seamus Heaney knew that if he visited the 'old man-killing parishes' [21] near Aarhus in Denmark, where Tollund Man was exhumed, he would feel 'lost, / Unhappy and at home'.[22] But we might hope that Sarah Lund's dedication to the exercise of reason is also part of the appeal of *The Killing*. Clearly, whether in Staffordshire or Yorkshire or some other part of our most secretive country, the material is there, if a poet can be found to deal with it.

I Wouldn't Start from Here

I concluded the previous lecture by suggesting that the collapse of politics into a popular culture of revenge could provide a major subject for the poet wishing to write history poems, to take the measure of the times – an opportunity which seems as yet untaken.

So where is the radical poetry of the present? To pursue this I need once more to move outside poetry to one of the adjacent literary forms. In Trevor Griffiths's 1974 play *The Party*, about the failure of the Left in Britain to seize the revolutionary moment that seemed to be offered by the events of 1968 else-where, there is an extended discussion involving John Tagg, a veteran Trotskyist, who eloquently diagnoses the ills of the left-wing intelligentsia and the emergent media class:

> You start from the presumption that only you are educated and sensitive enough to see how bad capitalist society is... Suddenly you lose contact – not with ideas, not with abstractions, concepts, because they're after all your stock-in-trade. You lose contact with the moral tap-roots of socialism. In an objective sense, you actually stop believing in a revolutionary perspective, in the possibility of a socialist society and the creation of socialist man. You see the difficulties, you see the complexities and contradictions, and you settle for those as a sort of game you can play with each other. Finally you learn to enjoy your pain; to need it, so that you have nothing to offer your bourgeois peers but a sort of moral exhaustion. You can't build socialism on fatigue, comrades... You've contracted the disease you're trying to cure.[1]

It's worth pointing out that when this play was first staged, at the National Theatre, the part of Tagg was played by Sir Laurence Olivier, the greatest actor of the day, an establishment figure par excellence. This is perhaps a sign of the strange, disarming inclusiveness of English life, as well as of Olivier's ability to spot a wonderful oratorical set-piece. Strange also to try to overlay in the imagination Olivier's speech before the walls of Harfleur in his great wartime film of *Henry V* with Tagg's eloquent analysis of an impotence which he knows his words will not banish.

Tagg is condemned by other characters in the play, seen as 'a brutal shite underneath, with a fist where his mind used to be',[2] but his speeches are the closest thing this play – deliberately and ironically constructed as a closet piece, a talking-shop – comes to action (and to poetry), and his vision is compelling and poignant to many who will dissent from its beliefs and conclusions. His is the last flare of revolutionary obligation, soon to be discredited and extinguished (his model seems to have been Gerry Healy of the Workers' Revolutionary Party, who was indeed discredited), but in the play's period Tagg is something more than an eccentric survivor speaking a language that listeners can barely understand. His time, we are told nowadays, is long gone. There are no politics of the kind he represents, only a series of timid negotiations with the implacably voracious forces of capital.

Searching the immediately contemporary theatre for something related to *The Party*, the most prominent example is Lee Hall's *The Pitmen Painters*, about the Ashington Group of painters, a richly ambiguous and very funny depiction of aspiration and disappointment, a parable of the failure of the 1945 Labour Government to deliver fully on the hope of a fairer society before being narrowly defeated in the 1951 election (despite having more votes than the Conservatives). *The Pitmen Painters* was written for and developed by Newcastle's own Live Theatre. While writing this lecture I came across a newspaper advertisement for the play's recent transfer into the West End. As is usual, the advertisement featured approving quotations from press reviews. What was intriguing was the source of the extremely enthusiastic comments: *The Daily Telegraph, The Times, Mail on Sunday, The Daily Mail, Sunday Express, The Daily Express*. I think it's fair to say that we are not in *Socialist Worker* territory here. Can it be that all these critics have misunderstood the play? Lee Hall's own socialism presents itself –

like that of a writer he sometimes resembles, the late Alan Plater – in a genial, unthreatening way, as an extension of common sense and decent generosity of spirit (English virtues, we like to think), and (as is also true of *Billy Elliot*) in the context of something widely felt (though not by Hall himself) to be historical, done with and therefore free now to accumulate the sepia charm of the remote and impotent. And of course both plays focus on the struggle and success of an individual, whether this is Billy, the dancer, or Oliver Kilbourn, the most prominent of the pitmen painters. These plays are somehow, despite the author's clear intentions, enclosed and domesticated – recuperated, as a theorist might put it – by the very powers they oppose. Everyone remains inside the whale, or: this is the whale, nor are we out of it.

This lecture is being written on a Saturday when *The Guardian* runs its Books of the Year feature – brief comments on recommended reading from about thirty writers. Very few of them are poets and only three books of poetry get a mention. We might take this as a snapshot of poetry's marginality, its sombre character emphasised by its appearing in *The Guardian*, which of all the national newspapers is easily the most hospitable to poetry. The books mentioned are all, to use an unhelpful term, in the "mainstream". Coverage of poetry in *The Guardian* is often accompanied by markedly contrasting online comments which indicate that for some readers the paper features all the wrong material, and that there is a great submerged continent of experiment and innovation from which we could all get the benefit if things were not stitched up by a gang of cunning morons, producers of mainstream 'mince' et cetera. Well, maybe, though at times on the books blog we seem to be in the presence of new examples of what Douglas Dunn in 'Remembering Lunch' called 'manias without charm'[3] and 'integrity that has been lying around so long it has begun to stink'.[4]

Yet there is indeed an entire body of poetry which exists more or less underground – and I mean the serious sort, not necessarily the sort churned out in a fury of incompetence by some blogospheric eunuch-defying Malcolm and his two mates in various sock-smelling bedrooms in the Nuneaton area. This is variously called experimental, neo-modernist, innovatory and "real". To some of it there is a strong critical-theoretical element and a Marxist analysis of the need to re-make language in order to free it from the corrupting influence of capitalism. In some respects this strand (which is much more complex than there is space to suggest) runs in parallel with the American postmodern poetry which has been driven to break with "tradition" out of a sense that "tradition" has come to distort the realities of life after the Korean and Vietnam wars, and that thus it serves the interests of the military-industrial complex.

There is truth in this approach, to the extent that any poetry worth the name is always trying to make space for its own nature to flourish, but there is often an accompanying category error whereby poetic form itself is seen as at best an unwitting part of the larger political and economic conspiracy. The work of poets such as Douglas Dunn and Tony Harrison – claimants to tradition for radical ends – gives the lie to that. And as regards this phenomenon in England, as so often, there is a comic dimension to the matter, in that the avant-garde professes to despise "the mainstream" and its vulgar public life (such as it is) while seething with fury at being excluded from the rather faint limelight.

In a notorious comment in his introduction to the anthology *New British Poetry* (2004), Don Paterson concluded a damning assessment of the imaginative and formal poverty of the avant-garde (which he calls Postmoderns) by stating: 'the Mainstream insist on a talented minority, and a democracy of readership; the Postmoderns on an elite readership, and a democracy of talent'.[5] We might say that the difference he describes is between pessimism and contempt. It is worth noting that Paterson now publishes one of the most wide-ranging experimentalists of all, the Australian John Kinsella, presumably on the grounds that his work will bear artistic and critical scrutiny and prove to offer something rather more compelling than the obscurely insistent sense of exceptionalism and self-righteousness evinced by some of his contemporaries.

Geoffrey Hill, who is no one's idea of an Ampersand, remarked that difficult poetry is democratic in that it treats the audience as intelligent beings: amen to that. But there is a difference between difficulty, which offers a challenge to the reader's imagination, and the kind of obscurity which has less to do with substance than with signalling a superior exclusivity. Faced with political disappointment, the response of many poets of a left-wing persuasion has been to retire further into the bowels of the whale, to write and speak a language that the whale is not intended to understand, even supposing it were listening. Avant-gardism is nowadays often a kind of acceptance of defeat, the construction of an alternative world of discourse intended for a non-existent public, and at times revealing, as John Tagg puts it, 'a sort of moral exhaustion',[6] symptomatic of the disease for which the radical imagination was part of the intended cure.

Poets of the so-called "mainstream" are themselves wise to maintain a degree of pessimism. They may get nearly all the attention (whatever that consists of), but this really amounts to ten per cent of not much. Certainly, few poets have the audience or the public platform available to a writer such as Lee Hall, though most of them would be in broad sympathy with his politics. Perhaps only the Poet Laureate, Carol Ann Duffy, or Simon Armitage, have the same order of presence in the attention of the interested public. Neither can be accused of not trying to encourage the reading and enjoyment of poetry.

It is tempting to suggest that what we are witnessing in and through poetry is the break-up of England, a faintly audible accompaniment to the more widely noticed break-up of Britain which was foreseen some time ago by Tom Nairn and now seems to be going steadily ahead, as devolution tilts towards autonomy in Scotland and cross-border co-operation between Northern Ireland and the Republic. Can Wales be far behind? The very notion of Englishness seems of little use or value to many younger poets, though some are pursuing a more engaged line. In poetry this break-up is sometimes suggested by an intense regionalism, which is not at all the same thing as provincialism. It is a way of reading through place, and through the sensibility fostered by place, often a reading downwards and inwards (recalling Auden's landscape fidelities). It is often – in a familiar sense – celebratory and at the same time elegiac:

the poetry is somehow able to breathe the air of a past both real and imagined. It is not – as the avant-garde might seem to wish it to be – programmatic, but improvised out of the continuous day to day life of the imagination as it negotiates among the past, the present and the possible.

Two contrasting poets exemplify varieties of this tendency. Peter Bennet, a member of the Dunn / Harrison / Wainwright generation but only now beginning to receive due recognition, operates in a Northumberland of the mind in which ballad, legend, antiquarianism and supernatural intervention have created a kind of haunted simultaneity. Bennet chooses to work in a formally intricate style, with complex rhyme-patterns and a strong rhythmic drive which may at times disguise the real strangeness of his creations. A much younger poet, Tony Williams has applied his attention to his native ground – the Derbyshire Peak District and Sheffield – and in doing so promises to fulfil possibilities suggested by both Roy Fisher and Jeffrey Wainwright, while bringing his own idiosyncrasy and frequently comic spirit to bear. See for example 'The Matlock Elegies'. Here Williams relocates Rilke's *Duino Elegies* from the storm-tossed Schloss Duino overlooking the Adriatic to the prim Derbyshire spa town of Matlock. See also the extraordinary title-poem of his first collection, *At the Corner of Arundel Lane and Charles Street*.

The core readership of poetry will seek these writers out. But what of the wider public presence of poetry? The role of the poet laureate attracts attention and an inarticulate pressure of not wholly serious expectation, and it must take a strong artistic will in order to keep open the lines of communication between the poet and her original imaginative life. Carol Ann Duffy's recent collection *The Bees* suggests that she is doing so. Yet there are parts of the book when a sense of obligation seems to reveal itself in an effort to 'speak for England' which is both wholly serious and at the same time less than wholly persuasive, perhaps because its very generosity of spirit denies it a certain critical leverage.

It is often thought that to be Poet Laureate does damage to a poet's work, perhaps by introducing the element of compromise required by ceremony and a sense of obligation. The evidence is mixed, though, and recently quite encouraging. One or two of Ted Hughes's laureate poems are very interesting in their own right; Andrew Motion managed to keep an imaginative space for his own work. What about Duffy?

The Bees is arguably her most interesting book since *Mean Time* (1993). The best work is concise, with a rich musical authority that brings some of the poems close to song. Yet whilst there are poems here about history and politics (the poem called 'Politics' sees that compromised art as a curse, as the opposite of poetry), the sense of the contemporary is often in abeyance. Duffy has instead drawn on a thread of tradition that leads back through poets such as Charles Causley, Walter de la Mare and Christina Rossetti to suggest that while poetry is much occupied by time it is, in a sense, timeless. The bee motif, which suggests language, collective effort, work and calm, helps to orchestrate the collection along these lines. Older readers might be reminded of De la Mare's classic anthology for the young, *Come Hither*, or of James Reeves's multi-volume *The Rhyming River*, where poems are definitely poems, recognisable to those made uneasy or cross by "modern poetry" (even though "modern poetry" is now at least a century old). John Ashbery it ain't. This is a very difficult and risky move. Were Duffy not so musically alert the result would be sentimental and anachronistic. As it is, she approaches the borders of these conditions but for the most part veers skilfully away.

'John Barleycorn', which draws on the memory of the folk song, seeks to use the death and resurrection of the barley to represent an unquenchable national spirit. This is currently threatened by the rapid closure of thousands of pubs under the general pressure of economic recession and the particular destructive force of supermarkets selling cut-price drink. A (perhaps) unintended effect of this is to erode the conversational life that goes on, however ignorantly and repetitively, in pubs, thus increasing an air of isolation already encouraged by paranoia about security. If anything could justify Margaret Thatcher's disbelief in 'society' it might be this development. Of a tavern, Dr Johnson said: 'wine there exhilarates my spirits, and prompts me to free conversation and an interchange of discourse with those whom I most love: I dogmatise and am contradicted, and in this conflict of opinion and sentiments I find delight'. [7] For how much longer? Duffy writes:

Britain's soul, as the crow flies so flew he.
I saw him in the Hollybush, the Yew Tree,
the Royal Oak, the Ivy Bush, the Linden.
I saw him in the Forester, the Woodman.
He history, I saw him in the Wellington, the Nelson,
Greyfriars Bobby, Wicked Lady, Bishop's Finger.
I saw him in the Ship, the Golden Fleece, the Flask
the Railway Inn, the Robin Hood and Little John,
my green man, legend strong, re-born, John Barleycorn. [8]

This is the poem as pub crawl, though in the noble cause of the common life. John Barleycorn travels through Britain, we hear, although the whole thing may strike dissenters (including some of Duffy's fellow Scots) as suspiciously like Merrie England, history as myth, history with the politics taken out, an approach vulnerable to less benign forms of patriotism than the one Duffy mildly commends. 'Britain' and 'British', as was remarked earlier, are difficult terms to use with conviction these days.

The old song 'John Barleycorn' itself has an anarchic, subversive note – the fruit of the barley overturns authority and order and yet life is insupportable without it. And in another dimension of the song its subject is human sacrifice – corn-gods, death, resurrection, renewed subjection – a pattern which both underlies Christianity and describes the daily course of the national disease which to many observers The Drink has become. To adapt William Empson, himself no stranger to conviviality, it is an ambiguous gift, 'as what gods give must be', [9] the god of drink being either Dionysos or Diageo, depending who you ask.

The depiction of barleycorn as a benign element of commonality is only half the story. It leads us back to sentimental nationalism of the kind embodied in G.K. Chesterton's 'rolling English drunkard' on 'the rolling English road' [10] and Chaz and Dave's boozy anthem: 'I'm all right, I don't care, / I've got me beer in the sideboard there.' Hogarth's two pictures – 'Gin Lane' and 'Beer Street' saw beer as the salvation of the poor, but it would be more accurate to say that beer is a consolation, one with the dangerous edge on show in football crowds and town centres on Saturday nights. The intensity of alcohol abuse does really seem to speak for England – an England of discontent and aimlessness, in which national pride often finds a curdled racist expression. The reason why Duffy's very interesting poem somehow undoes itself is that the past it summons as witness is static. Things have moved on, and to fail to acknowledge this may be to succumb to the temptations of Heritage, which is made of the complacency of the rulers and the impotence of the ruled.

A more compelling account of The Drink appears in Tim Binding's strangely underrated novel, *Anthem*, which depicts the English at war from 1939-45 to the Falklands in 1982 and also takes in the King's Cross fire. Fire and water are the book's elements, and they combine as firewater in the orgiastic celebrations in London pubs on VE night 1945. The fiery, ungovernable core of England is revealed – as it is in Jez Butterworth's play *Jerusalem*, which opens with the hero Johnny Byron, Lord of Misrule, suffering a volcanic hangover – 'Look, don't start – I've got a throbber on' [11] – and can be interpreted as marking the last stand of anarchic Englishness (under the flag of Wessex) in the face of homogenising authority. This doomed struggle was in a sense acted out on a larger stage in the recent riots, an event whose reception suggested that England suffers a kind of collective amnesia, though in this case (for a change) induced not by alcohol but by sobriety. On sober reflection, authorities and respectable citizens alike prefer to treat the riots as unique or at least extremely rare, or failing that, as uncharacteristic, when in fact the history of the capital in particular shows it to be a tinder box of mass discontent, inchoate or otherwise, driven by religion, race, economics and the hooligan juice of the day, breaking out into fiery disorder at frequent intervals from the peasants' revolt to the Fascist marches of the 1930s and the Poll Tax riots of the 1980s. As Simon Armitage has commented, 'People don't do that for no reason.' For Roy Fisher, Birmingham is a furnace; but so, often, is the larger England, the furnace of an English making and unmaking.

A poetic admirer of Fisher is the Hull-based poet Peter Didsbury, whose poem 'In Britain' (by which, again, he seems to mean England) gives a joyfully vulgar account of an early medieval society devoting an evening to the pleasures of the table. The absence of main verbs in Didsbury's poem, and thus of a definite or completed time sequence, seems to avoid Duffy's problems: this is not nostalgia. This is something else.

> The guests at their conversation,
> abundance of dogs and pigs in these islands.
> The guests at their serious business, lying in pools.
> The stories, farting and belching across the puddled boards.
> The gross imaginations, bulging with viscera.
> The heads full of stories, the stories thwacked like bladders.
> The stories steaming in time to the music.
> The stories, chewed like lumps of gristle.
> The stories describing extravagant herds.
> The stories, reasons for killing each other.[12]

Hard to tell the human from the beast here, hard not to wonder if the 'extravagant herds' are not now wandering through Bluewater or Trafford Park or the Metro Centre or the new Westfield shopping centre next door to the site of the 2012 Olympics, protected by pilotless aerial drones of the kind used to such effect in Afghanistan and Pakistan.

In his gross comedy, Didsbury recalls Ted Hughes's observation of the bloodthirsty psychopath waiting his time in the mind of a Yorkshireman, and he also offers a ripely ignoble vision of the world that legend has made Arthurian. The poet who may prove to be Hughes's most persuasive successor, Simon Armitage, has made a version of the great Arthurian poem, *Sir Gawain and the Green Knight* – a work that seems to offer as though by direct imaginative injection a medieval vision of Englishness as place where the real and the fabulous stand either side of a fork in the forest trail. Hughes himself used a quotation from *Gawain* as the epigraph to his 1967 collection *Wodwo* (incidentally the first book of poems I owned) which is named after a wood-spirit referred to by the Gawain poet as Sir Gawain wanders in the fastness of the Wirral and beyond, seeking the Green Knight's castle:

Sumwhyle wyth wormez he werrez, and with wolues als,
Sumwhyle wyth wodwos, þat woned in þe knarrez,
Boþe wyth bullez and berez, and borez oþerquyle,
And etaynez, þat hym anelede of þe heȝe felle; [13]

(Etaynez are giants and ogres, perhaps rather like today's
nightclub doormen or shopping mall security.) Gawain's journey
to his encounter with the Green Knight, via dalliance with the
Lady, takes us not so much off the map as *into* it, to the deep
original there-and-not-there England whose traces persist into
the work of Hardy, Housman and Edward Thomas. A famous
edition of *Sir Gawain*, still in use, was co-edited by J.R.R.
Tolkien, whose major non-academic work, *The Lord of the Rings*,
attempts a complete mythological world drawing on Norse and
other linguistic sources. To some readers, wherever else Middle
Earth may be, it is clearly England, with the Shire perhaps
located in the Welsh borders and the great River Anduin taking
the place of the Severn, across which the bestial Orcs come
swarming out of the blasted furnace-world of Birmingham, or
Mordor. Tolkien's is an elegiac work, for though order is restored
and the rightful king acclaimed, the wounded hero, Frodo, is
drawn to the Grey Havens, to leave this world.

This England, then, is both here and elsewhere (or as Jeff
Beck succinctly put it, 'everywhere and nowhere, baby'), for
Tolkien, for the *Gawain* poet, for Hughes as he reaches deep
into Elmet and into the pre-human consciousness of the wodwo,
the wood-spirit, in the poem of the same name. Reaching back
towards a point before utterance, before language which loves
the world has developed the tools to confine it, brings us close to
Auden's stony saga-landscape once more. All these conceptions
seem to depend on an unknowable but necessary ur-world
which by turns governs, enchants and excludes and ratifies us.
There is something of this appeal behind Simon Armitage's
new version of *The Death of King Arthur*, whose publication
follows his recent comments about the 'cracks' in contemporary
English society, his detection of 'a whiff of rot' [14] and suggestion
that 'the West, maybe it's over'. [15] These intimations of mood, he
noted, are likely to make themselves present even in apparently
remote contexts – 'Even if you're only writing about a teapot', [16]

as he put it – or about the death of King Arthur, an undertaking that – as has been repeatedly apparent in the work referred to in these lectures – seems both celebratory and elegiac. As Auden wrote: 'The glacier knocks in the cupboard, / The desert sighs in the bed, / And the crack in the tea-cup opens / A lane to the land of the dead.' [17]

The trajectory of the poet is not always this direct. Jo Shapcott's work is less directly concerned with the 'condition of England' than that of some other poets, but a sense of the fragility of familiar categories does take memorable form in the title poem from *Phrase Book*, a litany of phrases rich in no longer viable cultural assumptions, including, most famously, those spelt out in the closing stanza:

> Where is the British Consulate? Please explain.
> What does it mean? What must I do? Where
> can I find? What have I done? I have done
> nothing. Let me pass, please. I am an Englishwoman. [18]

You can almost hear the ground of her being dissolving under the speaker's feet, the power having long since drained away, leaving what in another famous example, she refers to as 'the complicated shame of Englishness'. [19] This phrase occurs in the poem 'A Letter to Dennis', an elegy addressed to the television playwright Dennis Potter who, like Shapcott, had his roots in the Forest of Dean. This western part of Gloucestershire, deep in the borders, is one of those places of the margin and the edge which seems especially English almost for those reasons. It also has a history of revolt and riot by the Foresters in defence of their rights against enclosure and other incursions of moneyed authority. Potter himself, as we know, was by nature rebellious, to put it mildly: 'The point,' Shapcott goes on, 'is how to find a use for fury, / as you have taught, old father, / my old butt, wherever you are.' [20] Referring to the painful skin complaint of psoriasis by which Potter was afflicted (and which he memorably wrote about in *The Singing Detective*), Shapcott suggests a fundamental complication at the heart of the sense of Englishness: Potter comes to embody both its disease and its remedy, imagined in grotesquely erotic terms, 'still raucous and rejoicing / in the most painful erection in heaven / which rises through its carapace of sores / and cracking skin to sing in English'.[21] Dissent will only embed the dissenter deeper in the state of Englishness.

Even alienation can be a form of belonging – or at least that seems to one of the suggestions made by Paul Farley's poem 'From a Weekend First'. The narrator, who seems quite akin to the poet, engages in the quintessentially English activity of staring out of the window of a train, as dusk gathers:

> One for the money. Arrangements in green and grey
> from the window of an empty dining-car.
> No takers for this Burgundy today
> apart from me. I'll raise a weighted stem
> to my homeland scattering by, be grateful for
> these easy-on-the-eye, Army & Navy
> surplus camouflage colours that seem
> to mask all trace of life and industry;
>
> a draft for the hidden dead, our forefathers,
> the landfills of the mind where they turned in
> with the plush and orange peel of yesteryear,
> used up and entertained and put to bed
> at last; to this view where everything seems to turn
> on the middle distance. Crematoria, multiplex
> way stations in the form of big sheds
> that house their promises of goods and sex;
>
> to the promise of a university town,
> its spires and playing fields.[22]

England, on this reading is both visibly present and impalpable, a set of impressions which time is continually overtaking, a place where the past and the dead are both dominant and impotent – among them the poets of the past: 'promises of goods and sex' quotes Larkin's 'Money', and the poem as a whole shadows 'The Whitsun Weddings'. As well as social observation, the narrator applies some interior scrutiny. He knows himself for the product of history, someone educated to be able to join the dots and make the links and apprehend the irony of the process that has 'elevated' him to this point – the point where he can afford the indulgence of paying an extra sum to sit in a First Class compartment at the weekend; to pay, it seems, for a passage of solitude, for no one else is visible either on the train or in the landscape it travels through. Fellow travellers may share a sense that the passing landscape is also mysteriously deserted, one often strongest when passing through industrial districts: there never seems to be anyone about, though presumably they're inside actually working – but it can feel as though England is a giant set for an episode of *The Avengers*, where the population were typically absent, dead or evil. There's a subtle modulation to Farley's poem, until we realise that we are as it were on the inside of a history poem whose missing term is politics: 'No border guards / will board at this station, no shakedown / relieve me of papers or contraband: / this is *England*.'[23] True, but why does it become necessary to imagine such alien constraints? Perhaps because other, more effective controls are already in place. There seems to be no course of action but to drink the *pinot noir* and passively invite the judgement of the dead, to whom the speaker's transient and illusory privilege may indeed make him look like a fool. There is, as they say, no getting away from it, from England, not even in solitude. 'You cannot leave England,' wrote Peter Porter, 'it turns / A planet majestically in the mind',[24] but it might take a comparative newcomer to feel precisely that way. Some may have no desire to get away from it, choosing to come to England and seek to embrace it. The Australian Porter was one such, never quite grasping the local peculiarities of the England beyond the M25, yet asking a very important question in his poem 'At the Castle Hotel, Taunton': 'but where do the people of England live?'[25] Well, one again, as they say, if you have to ask – because, of course, it's a secret even from the English themselves. The landscape seen from the train may be both truthful and weirdly inaccessible. Where is England and who would you have to be to feel as if you lived there?

'Shibboleth', the title-poem of the late Michael Donaghy's first collection, concerns the passwords American soldiers needed to identify themselves during the Ardennes conflict of late 1944. In this case the passwords were the names of the singing group, The Andrews Sisters:

> The morning of the first snowfall, I was shaving,
> Staring into a mirror nailed to a tree,
> Intoning the Christian names of the Andrews Sisters.
> 'Maxine, Laverne, Patty.'[26]

Imagine if those of us born in England were obliged to take the nationality text taken by those applying for citizenship. Would we pass? Are our preoccupations the same as those of the government and the BBC? Who is to judge? I remember hearing an item on the radio many years ago about how the BBC decided on the pronunciation of placenames. An example given was Slaithwaite near Huddersfield. BBC pronunciation favoured *Slaithwaite*, but the locals called it Slawit, so a compromise was sought by consulting a local figure of authority, the Church of England vicar, who favoured *Slathwaite*. As Donaghy showed, these could be vital distinctions. His poem in turn recalls Will Hay's wartime comedy *The Goose Steps Out*, in which Hay played the double of a German general and infiltrated a German spying school, where the students, including Peter Ustinov and Charles Hawtrey, wrestled with English pronunciations, tending to pronounce Slough as Sluff. It was explained to them that Slough was Slough. Of course, they'd have been buggered if they'd gone to Brough.

As well as to poets in general, these fictions of authenticity may be of special interest to immigrants – evidence of subjects and responses that the newcomer may want to internalise. George Szirtes's family escaped from Hungary when the Soviet Union crushed the Uprising in 1956. On beneficial effect of this ordeal was to make Szirtes wholly bilingual. He is fascinated by Englishness and participates wholeheartedly in it, even while bringing a distinct Hungarian inflection to his work. In some sense he is the man who knows too much. It is the mythology of the commonplace, the reification of the transient, that seems particularly to interest him. His immersion in English ordinariness – such as 'the soft green books of Dickson Carr. Ngaio Marsh and Christie', a memory of the long-gone green Penguin Crime novels – is so vivid because at one level he never quite believes in a world which is 'half pulp, half mysticism, school of Palmer'. While he knows the reified, talismanic England of 'Sid James, Diana Dors / Brylcreem and Phyllosan' better than most of the natives, he also knows how little it might take to undo it, because he has inhabited an equivalent everyday world elsewhere. In the residential courtyards of his native Budapest for example, potted plants and bicycles are found within hailing distance of murder, as in 'The Courtyards': 'There's always someone to consider, one / you have not thought of, one who lies alone, / or hangs, debagged, in one more public square'.[27] In this new context, the Billy Bunteresque 'debagged' adds a special chill. And recently Szirtes has not been alone in noticing an increase in anti-Semitism, a phenomenon the English would generally prefer to believe is really to be found elsewhere. But as Robert de Niro's character in *The Deer Hunter* says, trying to dispel a friend's illusions, 'This is this.'

I'll close this generally sombre survey with a younger poet, an optimist. Daljit Nagra was born here in 1965 to a family who came to England from the Punjab. He grew up in West London and Sheffield. Nagra's impact – he is the first British Asian poet to come to the forefront of attention – has something to do with his ability to convey the real complexity of the interactions of different ethnic groups as well between the generations within them. He shows us the assumptions and misunderstandings by which people are bedevilled, but also the fruitful augmentation of the idea of England, and of the English language itself. Nagra is also very funny, which doesn't hurt: he can, for example, write about his own mother accusing him of becoming a white man.

In 'Yobbos', from his first collection, *Look We Have Coming to Dover*, Nagra's speaker recalls sitting on the Tube and being abused by skinheads for reading '*Some Pakki shit like*'.[28] The ironies are several and painfully funny. Nagra, as mentioned, is British-born and of Bengali, not Pakistani descent, while the book he's reading would be counted as English Literature but is actually the *Collected Poems* of Paul Muldoon, an Irish poet born in the deeply ambiguous territory of Northern Ireland. It is a place where the word 'British' rather than English means something highly particular to the half of the community which claims it (a claim viewed with amused bafflement by many of the English whose historical fault everything seems to be and probably is). It is also the non-sectarian birthplace of a disproportionate amount of the best contemporary poetry in English. For the skinheads on the tube to bear all this in mind might be asking a little too much. Furthermore the narrator is not the

first to read Muldoon with a mixture of absorption and exasperation. He finds himself wanting to cry out: '*Well mate, this Paki's more British than that inde-/ cipherable, impossibly untranslatable //
sod of a Paddy – / only I don't*',[29] because that way (Cromwellian) madness lies. At the same time, Nagra has used an affectionate parody of Muldoon's rhyming.

The best of Nagra's debut, *Look We Have Coming to Dover*, crackles with this rueful, outraged humour and manages to dramatise the complexities of ethnicity and identity in a diasporic world. The verve and energy and startlingly vivid language are sustained in its successor, *Tippoo Sultan's Incredible White-Man-Eating Tiger Toy-Machine!!!* This is very much a book that deals with the way in which we're all in it together for the long run – whether we like it or realise it or not. Nagra's beguilingly direct and confident manner handles love poems and the melancholy comedy of a retelling of *Romeo and Juliet* as a problem of caste for Raju and Jaswinder, alongside rich and complex historical pieces. 'The Ascent of a Victorian Woman', allegedly from a journal, is a dramatic monologue about English travellers losing their bearings in Victorian India, while 'A Black History of the English-Speaking Peoples' finds the links between old empire and ex-colony to be complex and unbreakable even as their meanings shift for those living now. Those polar opposites Philip Larkin and Tony Harrison are both enlisted by allusion and precedent, while Nagra's charm and generosity of spirit issue both an invitation and a challenge.

The impression given by Nagra is that despite all the evidence to the contrary, England is a place yet to be created – a heartening view, if not an easy one for older English people to take on trust, given the habit of disappointment. But as Captain Picard would say, 'Make it so.' Perhaps then, in Douglas Dunn's words, 'Our grudges will look quaint and terrible'.[30] Perhaps. Good luck to the poet who travels the tube and the East Coast Line main line in hope.

NOTES

FIRST LECTURE
As Deep As England

1. Heinrich Heine, *The Harz Journey and Selected Prose* (London: Penguin, 1993; 2006) 'On the History of Religion and Philosophy in Germany', p. 255.

2. ibid p. 206.

3. William Shakespeare, *Richard II*, II. 1. 31-68.

4. G.K. Chesterton, 'The Secret People', line 2.

5. Peter Porter, *The Rest on the Flight: Selected Poems* (London: Picador Pan Macmillan, 2010), 'Fossil Gathering', p. 101.

6. Ted Hughes, *Collected Poems* (London: Faber and Faber, 2003), 'Pike', pp. 84-85.

7. T.S. Eliot, *Collected Poems 1909-1962* (London: Faber and Faber, 1936; 1974), 'Little Gidding', p. 222.

8. Alfred Corn, *The Poem's Heartbeat: A Manual of Prosody* (Port Townsend, WA, USA: Copper Canyon Press, 2008), p. 6.

9. W.H. Auden, *Collected Poems* (London: Faber and Faber, 2007), 'O where are you going?', pp. 59-60.

10. Philip Larkin, *Collected Poems* (London: The Marvell Press and Faber and Faber, 1988), 'Show Saturday', pp. 199-201.

11. ibid, p. 189.

12. W.H. Auden, *Collected Poems* (London: Faber and Faber, 2007), 'In Praise of Limestone', pp. 538-540.

13. Philip Larkin, *Collected Poems* (London: The Marvell Press and Faber and Faber, 1988), 'MCMXIV', p. 127.

14. Ted Hughes, *Collected Poems* (London: Faber and Faber, 2003), 'Dust As We Are', p. 753.

15. ibid, 'Thistles', p. 147.

16. Roy Fisher, *The Long and the Short of It: Poems 1955-2005* (Tarset: Bloodaxe Books, 2005), 'Texts for a Film 1: Talking to Camera', p. 285.

17. Geoffrey Hill, *Collected Poems* (London: Penguin, 1985), 'Funeral Music', p. 72.

18. William Wordsworth, 'The Solitary Reaper', line 19.

19. Roy Fisher, *The Long and the Short of It: Poems 1955-2005* (Tarset: Bloodaxe Books, 2005), 'It is Writing', p. 221.

20. ibid, 'For Realism', pp. 220-21.

21. Geoffrey Hill, *Collected Poems* (London: Penguin, 1985), 'Funeral Music', p. 72.

22. Michael Donaghy, *Collected Poems* (London: Picador, 2009), 'Black Ice and Rain', p. 124.

23. Roy Fisher, *The Long and the Short of It: Poems 1955-2005* (Tarset: Bloodaxe Books, 2005), 'From an English Sensibility', p. 251.

SECOND LECTURE
Enemies Within

1. Stephen Spender, 'Changeling: a Review of *Continuous: 50 Sonnets from "The School of Eloquence"* by Tony Harrison', in *The New York Review of Books*, 15 July 1982.

2. Thom Gunn, *Collected Poems* (London: Faber and Faber, 2003), 'My Sad Captains', p. 129; 'Claus von Stauffenberg', p. 111.

3. Jeffrey Wainwright, *Selected Poems* (Manchester: Carcanet, 1985), '1815', pp. 40-43

4. William Shakespeare, *Hamlet*, IV. 7. 166-83.

5. Karl Marx and Friedrich Engels, *Manifesto of the Communist Party* (1848), Chapter 1: Bourgeois and Proletarians.

6. Roger McGough, *In the Glassroom* (London: Cape, 1976), p.9.

7. William Shakespeare, *King Lear*, II. 3. 18.

8. William Shakespeare, *Richard II*, II. 1. 60.

9. Plautus (250-184 BC), Asinaria.

10. Philip Larkin, *Collected Poems*, ed. Anthony Thwaite (London: The Marvell Press and Faber and Faber, 1988), 'Toads' p. 89.

11. Tony Harrison, *Selected Poems* (London: Penguin, 2006), 'National Trust', p. 121.

12. ibid, 'On Not Being Milton', p. 112

13. Douglas Dunn, *Terry Street* (London: Faber and Faber, 1969), 'New Light on Terry Street', p. 14.

14. Tony Harrison, *Selected Poems* (London: Penguin, 2006), 'On Not Being Milton', p. 112

15. Richard Curtis, *The Faber Book of Parodies*, ed. Simon Brett (London: Faber and Faber, 1984), 'The Skinhead Hamlet'.

16. Douglas Dunn, *Barbarians* (London: Faber and Faber, 1979), 'Gardeners', pp. 17-18.

17. Peter Reading, *Collected Poems 1: Poems 1970-1984* (Newcastle upon Tyne: Bloodaxe Books, 1995), 'Duologues' 3, p. 100.

18. ibid.

19. James Fenton, *The Memory of War and Children in Exile: Poems 1968-1983* (Harmondsworth: Penguin, 1983), 'A Staffordshire Murderer'.

20. ibid.

21. Seamus Heaney, *Selected Poems 1965-1975* (London: Faber and Faber, 1980), 'Tollund Man', pp. 78-79.

22. ibid.

THIRD LECTURE
I Wouldn't Start from Here

1. Trevor Griffiths, *The Party* (London: Faber and Faber, 1974), p. 49.

2. ibid, p. 46.

3. Douglas Dunn, *Selected Poems* (London: Faber and Faber, 1986), pp. 173-76.

4. ibid.

5. *New British Poetry*, ed. Don Paterson & Charles Simic (St Paul, MN, USA: Graywolf Press, 2004), 'Introduction', p. xxxiii.

6. Trevor Griffiths, *The Party* (London: Faber and Faber, 1974), p. 49.

7. Sir John Hawkins, *Life of Samuel Johnson* (1778).

8. Carol Ann Duffy, *The Bees* (London: Picador, 2011), pp. 29-30.

9. William Empson, *Collected Poems* (London: Chatto & Windus, 1955; 1969), p. 32.

10. *The Collected Poems of G.K. Chesterton* (London: Palmer, 1927), 'The Rolling English Road'.

11. Jez Butterworth, *Jerusalem* (London: Nick Hern Books, 2009), p. 11.

12. Peter Didsbury, *Scenes from a Long Sleep: New and Collected Poems* (Tarset: Bloodaxe Books, 2003), 'In Britain', p. 202.

13. Ted Hughes, *Wodwo* (London: Faber and Faber, new ed. 1971).

14. John Harris's National Conversations: Simon Armitage (video interview) http://www.guardian.co.uk/books/video/2011/nov/07/simon-armitage-poetry-video-interview

15. ibid

16. ibid

17. W.H. Auden, *Collected Poems*, ed. Edward Mendelson (London: Faber and Faber, 1976; revised 1991), 'As I Walked Out One Evening', pp. 134-35.

18. Jo Shapcott, *Her Book: Poems 1988-1998* (London: Faber and Faber, 2000), 'Phrasebook', pp. 65-66.

19. ibid, 'A Letter to Dennis', p. 125.

20. ibid.

21. ibid.

22. Paul Farley, *The Ice Age* (London: Picador, 2002), 'From a Weekend First', pp. 3-4.

23. ibid.

24. Peter Porter, *The Last of England* (Oxford: OUP, 1970), 'The Last of England', p. 1.

25. Peter Porter, *Collected Poems* (Oxford: OUP, 1984), 'At the Castle Hotel, Taunton', p. 197.

26. Michael Donaghy, *Collected Poems* (London: Picador, 2009), p. 21.

27. George Szirtes, *New & Collected Poems* (Tarset: Bloodaxe Books, 2008), p. 127.

28. Daljit Nagra, *Look We Have Coming to Dover* (London: Faber and Faber, 2007).

29. ibid.

30. Douglas Dunn, *Selected Poems 1964-1983* (London: Faber and Faber, 1986), 'The Come-on', pp. 99-100.